A Painful Island Hope

ISBN: 9798836099350
Imprint: Independently published

For more information please email:
skfernandobooks@gmail.com

Authors Note

Thank you for choosing to read this book; I hope it moves something in your heart and maybe even resonates with you. The timeline written below is how the poems and prose that follows move. From an impersonal description of the current situation in my nation, to the personal thoughts of death and despair, followed by a confusing battle of the mind between giving up and moving forward. Finally reaching a state of equilibrium and honesty in needing help and fighting forward. This book is raw, it's real, and it's me.

When I first started writing this book, I was writing it with the sole purpose of trying to find cash in order to be able to gain an education and experience abroad. I was riddled with guilt for even aspiring to gain money using this book or even using this book purely for education, when many barely have food to eat.

One day I came to the realization that there should be no guilt in aspiring for more. When more means something as simple as learning in a better economy, should it not be encouraged? Why must I feel guilt when I work day in and day out only to be bogged down and passed over, simply because I didn't have a network of wealthy friends or rich parents to get money from. Am I not allowed to dream for more while I help my community in other ways?

One day when my miracle comes and I get the chance to learn, grow and see beyond the poverty, I know, I will do great things. We talk of many different billionaires born from poverty but no one ever connects it to the country they are born from or the connections they used in order to do so. Country of birth matters. Opportunity matters. A poor man in a developed nation has more access to opportunities for a better life if he only tires versus a middle class man in an undeveloped nation that tries hard with no thought of sleep.

One day I will achieve my dreams, be it from the funds of this book or be it because kind individuals helped me grow regardless of my race, religion and status. I will use my knowledge to reignite the sparks of a nation that is losing its own; to tell the ones that come after me, 'you can do it too.' And try to ensure that the ones who work hard and toil get a chance to live their dreams, regardless of which country they're born into.

I know now, life isn't easy. Life isn't meant to be easy. For if it was easy, I would never have had the urgency, the desperation, for money to fuel my dreams and see it come alive. Meaning I would never have known my capacity to write a book as such, be it messy as it is, these words would only have laid dormant in my head.

Background

This book contains the open thoughts of a girl living in a nation riddled with open corruption. A nation where dreaming big meant, to want a better education, but now, for many mean 3 meals a day. A nation where you could save for lifetimes and still be unable to afford the crippling tuition of an 'international student' if one were to aspire to be one. (Unless of course you were born with connections to the Royal Throne.)

Preface

April 2019

A seemingly normal year for the general population across the globe. A little island nation slowly healing from a civil war that lasted over 26 years with only a decade of peace between then and this date gets hit with something they never thought possible. (Again) A terrorist attack. What was meant to be a day of celebrating the risen king, for many became a day of mourning, fear and loss. As church bells rung on that fateful Easter Sunday, bombs exploded in churches filled with innocents. Many lives lost; many families broken, never to be the same again. A 20 year old girl, me, losses a friend.

March 2020

The coronavirus hits this island nation, and lockdown is imposed. Fighting waves of fear and anxiety, unvaccinated (at the time) that now, 21 year old girl goes to work, as being part of the media industry means you work even during a pandemic. Pay cuts enforced. Family business stands still as the hospitality industry crashes and loans taken to build mini lofts lay unpaid. Father's debt grows higher. Dipping into college savings to keep the family fed, she goes on.

April 2021

There seems to be a light. Lockdown eases and covid-19 cases drop. Even with pay cuts still in place, there seems to be hope for a slightly better life. At 22 years old, holding 3 odd jobs, college savings slowly reaching 2019 levels. Still far off from the target goal which seemed to keep growing as the years go on. (For aspiring 'international' students, cost of education rises year on year) With faith that things will work its way out if she just kept working hard towards her goal. She goes on.

January 2022

Prices of some essentials increase. Pay cuts no longer in place. The increase bearable. Funds towards education halted and put towards helping the growing debt of her parents.

March 2022

13 hour power cuts imposed. 2 jobs lost. Pay cuts back in place. At 23 being unable to afford basic necessities, not due to a lack of hard work or trying, but simply because the economy has failed; her nations leaders failed, breaks her up piece by piece. Prices of basic essentials seem to increase every week. The family business once again begins to run dry. College savings almost nonexistent, she has no choice but to clean it out in order to be able to purchase simple essentials like rice, the staple of her nation. One parent falls ill, but medicines are no longer in stock. No gas to cook. No petrol for vehicles to run.

No medicine. No basic essentials. Exorbitant prices in a short span of time that kept rising causes dread and hopelessness to creep in.

April 2022

Frustrated and angry, a group of innocent people, protest in front of their president's house. Knowing who brought their island nation to the point of bankruptcy, they cry out in pain. Staged/planned or merely a burst of anger in a few protestors cause an escalation with public property damaged at the site. Emergency laws enforced. Curfew imposed. There seemed to be no moment for her to breathe between working, house work; standing in cues for gas or milk powder. Like a silent serpent, hopelessness takes over her. The ugly head of depression rears its head high and drowns her. Unable to keep up with the news that seemed to turn from bad to worse every time she looks at it, she feels the strings of death close. Why live when there's no hope? Why go on when you have no money, not to fuel your dreams, but to even sustain yourself? The cost of her dream of gaining a better education rising, while her nation's currency deprecates with a failing economy. The family dynasty in power continuing to steal from the people in broad daylight. Suicide now on the table, she breaks away from friendships to ease the burden of taking her own life. The push and pull between living a life filled with sorrow and a peaceful death overwhelm her mind. Choosing to hang on because of her family she drags her beaten mind on, day in and day out.

May 2022

State instigated violence at peaceful demonstrations of protest against the tyranny of a ruling family that did nothing and continues to do nothing to ease the economic downturn cause the nation to go into another downward spiral. Nothing seems to stabilize. Justice for her people nowhere in the cards of the ones in power. A news headline reads, "A father loses his 2 day old daughter because he couldn't find fuel". Where's the hope? Cynical at how the aid from the international community will be used, she watches on as her country spirals along with her thin thread of sanity. She begins to wonder if mental health even exists. Can it even be considered important when you don't even have the luxury of uninterrupted electricity? When no semblance of justice can be seen?

An
Economic
Journey

They came as one of us

Whispering promises of hope, glory and triumph

Won us a war but kept us divided

Silenced those that dared go against

Took what was meant for our country's healing

Lined up the pockets of their own

Bought off any remaining

It's okay, many in our nation say

He won us the war

-       ***Not one of us?***

Once again they rose up under the veils of crisis
A need for a leader, a leader battle tested, born
The majority fall once again into their web
Like a crooked beauty, a 69 majority
Family placed in power
Books cooked
Pockets lined.

-        ***Unintentional Rebirth?***

Unchecked, unopposed

They ride like movie stars, in luxury

Eat like hungry lions, in luxury

Sleep like kings in luxury

A luxury the majority has never known before

A luxury stolen from the very people they were

meant to serve

A luxury paid for, by the blood of the innocent

-        ***Blood Money?***

They watch from the comfort of their thrones
While the ones they're meant to lead, bleed

Feast like they Gods of Egypt
While the people cry out in hunger

Steal funds meant for aid, for their own gain
While the people die without basic medicine
While the people mourn in despair

-        ***Ignorance is Bliss?***

They line their pockets

Shut out; ignore the people

Silence those that dare go against

Desperation is only for those whose hearts still beat

Fear exists only in the eyes of ones that feel

Not for those drunk on power

With hearts cold as ice

Eyes fixed on green paper

-        ***Green Tunnel Vision?***

Living it up, like they kings of North
Plight of the people ignored
Like they pests beyond the wall

The city falls apart underneath
Cracks seen across the land
But as long as their castle is stacked
A crisis, it is not

-        ***Like Kings of the North?***

Enough is enough
People take to the streets
With brokenness fueling their feet
Fear for their children, driving their haunted minds
Desperation filling their empty bellies
A blurry line between what's right and need

-        *Is there a line?*

Extremists they call them

Extremists? Maybe?

A son who struggles to study by candle light

A daughter who stands in cues for gas to cook

Only to go back home, empty handed for days

A mother who has to choose between eating a

meal and walking home

A father who works day and night only to be

unable to afford rent

All contemplating death

Those are the kind of people they call extremists

-        ***What's in a label?***

They're just doing their job
They too need that job to clothe their children
To try and fill the empty bellies of their own at
home
Are they to lose their income on a chance at
freedom?

A gamble

To see all sides of the story isn't always a blessing
Right now it's a curse
Out of a job
Family starving at home
Suffering in the heat like never before
Clouded by grief and pain
Desperation at the forefront of all actions

You need release
You act out in frustration having nothing left
It's understood
It's adorned
It's accepted
The ones against you, on the other side

My friend, they are not 'all' against you

Some yes, they do follow blindly like many did
Hitler
Others, now the many
Have no choice

Peacefully protest you may
Openly you may
Aggressively you may not

For in the end where you see your pain and your
families grief
They too see their own
Like two sides of a twisted, blood filled blade

-        ***Police aren't truly always brutal?***

How I wish we didn't have to feel
But we must
For that is what makes you different from them
From those that oppress us all

Two similar yet different stories
Bonded together like two sides of the same coin
They are not against you my friend
They are for you

Until you decide, grace is not the way to go
Until you decide to light a fire
Throw the first stone
Aggression is not the answer

Be loud, be boisterous
Dance, scream and sing
You have your rights

But my friend, do not harm that which is not yours

For they will be forced to act

Be it out of fear of losing of their job

Or be it out of possible starvation of their own
family

Or simply out of duty

You may not lose against them

But your future generations will.

-        ***Two Sides of the Law?***

A battle hero no longer required

A war criminal unnecessary
They, the people get back on the streets
The red scarfs, playing them for fools
Running around in circles
No answer given
Buying time, maybe?
What comes next?
The people stay on the streets
One demand chanted across the island

Send the crooked reds, home.

-        *A Joker or a Fool?*

Personal
Journey

I want to escape
I want to run away
Momentarily, my emotions get the best of me

People tell me *"guard my heart"*
"Don't let your emotions get the best of you"
But why not?

They tell us we must feel for other people
Empathize with them
But when it comes to our emotions, we mustn't let
it show

"Bear with it and move on"
"Everyone is going through the same"

Ah, but are they?

The people know the red scarfs are different
You know, they have stolen funds
I know, they keep looting my nation

So why must we keep quiet?
Why should I not let my emotions run wild?
Should I sit at home in silence and let the crooked
swim free?

-        ***Feel but don't?***

God do you not hear me?
Do you not see my tears or hear my cries?
Every night I cry myself to sleep
The exhaustion of the day and tears lull my mind to
sleep

I want to die.
Every day I wake up wondering, 'why?'

I'm tired.
I'm tired and broken beyond repair
I fall to edge of death everyday but keep coming
back
My stupid mind, why?
Why am I still alive?
Why will you not let me die?

-                              ***Unanswered why's?***

Pills, my body spits out

A blade too obvious

I want to die

Universe won't you let me?

You give me a hope, years away

A hope that keeps shaking

Every day I come back from an almost death

Let me die

Finish this

Must I suffer just so others may not cry?

-        **Not so suicidal?**

I wish, I never wake up to see another morn

Every dawn, I wish, I never woke

And yet I continue to live

I choose to wake up, work and live

Cowardice?

Fear of dying?

No.

Simply a trust that every cloud has a lining

Mine may not be silver

It may not be gold

But it has a lining and I can fight my mind, body and soul

Till one day that lining is clear as day

-      ***A lining exists?***

They'll never understand
The ones that have loving parents
The ones that get hugs from their parents

I am one that no one understands
I have not met anyone that feels the way I do
All stories seem to end with happy endings
With parents understanding their children
Mine are not the same
Every night I wish for a death that never comes
Death to my emotions
So I may never feel again but keep on living
What does that say about me?
A semi-fighter?
A half-baker?

- Death to Emotions?

No longer do I wish for a quick escape

That girl I buried deep within

That girl I will eradicate

Life is for everyone

But living is not

Why take your life without having truly lived

-        *For who is 'living?'*

Hope can be
Painful

An end to this misery

An end to this pain

An end to the state inflicted trauma

Remains to be seen

Watching as people die in cues

Watching as a mother struggles to feed her young

Dreaming of a better tomorrow

Working harder than the day before

Only to collect less than the day before

Survivors

Fighters

Pushing on in faith

-        ***Push on in Faith?***

Wanting; waiting for redemption
That only a miracle can bring

An end to this misery unseen
An end to this pain unheard
An end to this state inflicted trauma near impossible

But that's the cruel beauty of it

At the end of the line
At the end of yourself
At the final stretch
When your legs shake from running
When your mind starts shutting down
When your heart feels like it will burst at any
second

If you stick it out
Crawl when your legs have given away
On the last leg of battery, of your mind
When the blood begins to reach your ears

You will find more of you
A stronger you
One you never would have discovered had you
been sheltered

That's the cruel beauty of life isn't it?
To find yourself, you first must be lost

-        ***Lost, to be Found?***

I wish

For strength to keep fighting

To fight for myself

To fight for the years I'm losing in this crisis

To fight now, so I may rest in the years to come

I wish

For abundance

Abundance in wealth, not so that I may prosper
alone

But so one day I may see my parents retire

Abundance in grace, for all those who've jumped
ship and given up

I wish

For peace

Peace within my nation

Peace in the hearts of every man, woman and child

I wish for a lot, don't I?

But when you've tried everything
Gone down every path
Exhausted every option
You're left with wishes to hold onto while you toil
another day

\-   ***What's in a wish?***

Why do we mourn when one dies?

Shouldn't we celebrate a life lived instead?

Why do we spend money on flowers for the dead?

Should we not have spent it while they lived,

instead?

Why is it that we wait for a tragedy, to show our

humanity?

Should we not show compassion regardless?

-　　　　***Wasting on Death?***

Faith broken

Body bruised

Mind shattered

Future uncertain

Hope dwindling

Heart tears itself apart

And yet, here I stand

Here we stand

Because even

Faithless, hopeless, broken, bruised and

shattered

I know I must

We know we must

For silence means they won
And I won't let them win

We won't let them win

I've fought too hard

We've fought too hard

Shed too many tears
Lost too much
To back down now
Until it's finished
Until justice is served
Or my time on Earth is up
Only then will I rest

We will rest

Knowing I did my best

Knowing we did our best

To help the cause
Be part of the charge

Part of the change

-              ***Is giving up even an option?***

Sneak Peak

(From another book by S.K. Fernando
- currently in the making)

The battle for her body, unwinnable
Burning flames in her mind, uncontrollable
Tears in her soul, unamendable
Each step forward
Creating a pain unbearable
New bruises created, as old wounds healed

Even with foundations cracked, destroyed and
unrecognizable
Only she, herself as cheerleader by her side

She ran, she walked, crawled on
For she believed, there was more

More people to touch
More stories to shape
More molds to break

Even at the cost of self
It was a life that seemed to break her, more than
make her
But it didn't matter, for she knew no different

-        *There's always more.*

Acknowledgements

Firstly I want to thank, you, for reading my first ever official book! You are now part of my journey in this thing we call life.

A big thank you, to Sherry, who years ago once told me my journal will turn into song; for trusting me with her life journey and in turn inspiring me to be present, real and tangible. You along with Patrick will always have a piece of my heart for your tenderness and kindness towards me regardless of age, time and miles between us.

Finally thank you, to everyone I consider family both in blood and by choice. As many of you, even with miles between us, you've encouraged me and never given up on me. I consider you alien, for loving me through my mess as I journey.

Extra

If you would like to be privy to more updates, do send us your email address by filling in the form available at the link below.

https://forms.gle/kqGsbpg6Rp1sNzVE9

If you would like to donate towards my further education (beyond what you've already given me through royalties by purchasing this book) please feel free to visit the GoFundMe link below.

Thank you!

https://gofund.me/d5bdf22b

Instagram

@s.k.fernandobooks

A Painful
Island
Hope

9 798836 099350